THEN & NOW

SACRAMENTO

Capitol Avenue was originally known as M Street. From 1912 to 1940, it was the route of Sacramento Northern interurban trains. From 1926 to 1964, M Street was also U.S. Route 40. Both crossed the Sacramento River via the M Street Bridge and Tower Bridge (on the cover). The California state capitol building dominates the landscape in this *c.* 1950 photograph. Today high-rise buildings and state offices dominate Capitol Avenue, and the neighborhood in the foreground is gone. (Sacramento Archives and Museum Collection Center.)

THEN & NOW

SACRAMENTO

William Burg

Dedicated to my great aunt, Helen Yast, who told me I should write more often.

Copyright © 2007 by William Burg
ISBN 978-0-7385-5900-1

Library of Congress control number: 2008922669

Published by Arcadia Publishing
Charleston SC, Chicago IL, Portsmouth NH, San Francisco CA

Printed in the United States of America

For all general information contact Arcadia Publishing at:
Telephone 843-853-2070
Fax 843-853-0044
E-mail sales@arcadiapublishing.com
For customer service and orders:
Toll-Free 1-888-313-2665

Visit us on the Internet at www.arcadiapublishing.com

ON THE FRONT COVER: The M Street Bridge, completed in 1911, allowed interurban passenger trains, freight trains, and streetcars operated by Northern Electric to cross the Sacramento River. It was replaced by the Tower Bridge, a Streamline Moderne vertical lift bridge, in 1935. Trains crossed the Tower Bridge until the early 1960s. The bridge also had four automobile lanes. Today the Tower Bridge is one of Sacramento's most recognizable landmarks. (Historic photograph: Sacramento Archives and Museum Collection Center. Modern photograph: William Burg.)

ON THE BACK COVER: K Street was home to many of Sacramento's movie theaters, department stores, and hotels. On September 14, 1946, the marquee of the Hippodrome Theatre (right) collapsed, killing one person and injuring three others. The theater was closed for three years after the accident. It finally reopened as the Crest Theatre on October 6, 1949, and is still in operation today. (Sacramento Archives and Museum Collection Center.)

CONTENTS

ACKNOWLEDGMENTS

The historic photographs in this book were provided by the Sacramento Archives and Museum Collection Center (SAMCC). SAMCC is the main repository of Sacramento's history in photographs, documents, artifacts, and records of all kinds. However, this amazing collection would be unmanageable and inaccessible without the work of archivists. They hold a special place in the hearts of all historians. Archivists organize, preserve, store, and make available the information that allows historians to write books, formulate theories, and argue with each other over what it all means.

The archivists of SAMCC are the ones who make the treasure hunts of historians, both amateur and professional, far more likely to strike gold. Archivist Carson Hendricks provided invaluable support, advice, suggestions, and time to create this book, in addition to scanning the multitude of photographs I selected. Archivist Patricia Johnson also helped by presenting me with piles of photographs from little-known corners of the SAMCC vault. Thanks also to Marcia Eymann, SAMCC manager, for agreeing to make this project possible. The entire staff of SAMCC shares a passion for their work, extensive knowledge, and enormous patience with the waves of historians and students who come to SAMCC seeking golden nuggets of Sacramento history.

Additional primary research for this volume was done at the Sacramento Central Library's Sacramento Room, the California State Library's California Room, and the Sacramento State University Library. All contemporary photographs were taken by the author.

Thanks to the organizations that allowed me access to their rooftops to recreate aerial photographs without having to rent an airplane. Those organizations include Thomas Enterprises, SacJet, and Mike Sickels of the Sacramento Discovery Museum Gold Rush History Center. Thanks also to my editor, John Poultney, for his confidence in my abilities. Finally, thanks to my wife Vivian for her support, encouragement, and inspiration.

INTRODUCTION

During the Gold Rush, when gold seekers reached Sacramento they stopped only long enough to buy tools and provisions before heading into the gold country. When they ran low on provisions, they returned to Sacramento to resupply, to seek entertainment and a hot meal, and sometimes to seek work when gold proved too elusive. Most who came to Sacramento sought wealth in the goldfields. A few realized that the best way to acquire gold was to have gold miners bring it to them in exchange for shovels, eggs, and whiskey. Men like Sam Brannan, Benjamin Franklin Hastings, Peter Burnett, Collis P. Huntington, Charles Crocker, Leland Stanford, and Mark Hopkins started their fortunes as Gold Rush businessmen, selling everything from dry goods to plots of land. Doing business in this frontier environment required sharp wits, a ruthless disposition, and tireless effort. In this economic crucible, amateur businessmen like John Sutter and his young son John Sutter Jr. were no competition at all. Within a few years of the start of the Gold Rush, both left the city they had helped to create.

Sacramento's prime location as a center for trade and transportation during the Gold Rush was so important that matters like the valley's annual floods were secondary to the needs of commerce. Rather than move to higher ground, Sacramento's citizens built levees and elevated downtown streets to keep the town above water. Several attempts to establish new communities above flood level, including Norristown, Hoboken, and New Sacramento, lasted only until flooding subsided. When the original levees and street raisings proved insufficient, Sacramentans built stronger levees and raised the streets higher. By 1869, the majority of Sacramento's downtown core was above the flood waters, but additional street raising work continued until 1873. Street raising also reduced the risks of water-borne illnesses like cholera, which had ravaged the city in 1850.

Another milestone achieved in 1869 was the completion of the Central Pacific Railroad. The selection of its terminus in Sacramento was due to the successful lobbying efforts of the same entrepreneurs, including Huntington, Crocker, Stanford, and Hopkins, who made their fortunes during the Gold Rush. Invited by Crocker, 12,000 Chinese laborers built the railroad. These workers came to Sacramento seeking employment, not easy riches in the gold country. In the following decades, immigrants from around the world came seeking the same promise of work, eventually making Sacramento one of the most diverse cities in America. The Central Pacific, later known as the Southern Pacific Railroad, grew to become the dominant economic and political power in California.

A third achievement of 1869 was the occupation of California's new state capitol building, although construction was not complete until 1874. Many of that same group of ambitious Gold Rush merchants became politicians. Some, like Leland Stanford and Peter Burnett, even reached the rank of governor. Sacramento has maintained its role as the seat of California government since 1854, aside from the winter and spring of 1862, when floods forced the legislature to relocate to San Francisco. This was no small feat, considering the efforts made by other California cities to move the capital out of Sacramento.

Sacramento was never a quiet farming town or a bucolic village. It was born a city and attained regional and national importance within a few years of its founding. After 20 years of dramatic change, including political battles, monumental works of labor, riots, epidemics, fires, and floods, Sacramento settled down and went to work.

The working city included agricultural processing, heavy industry, transportation, and government. Farmers brought the bounty of the Central Valley to Sacramento for processing into flour, canned goods, beer, and wine. Raw materials from the Sierra Nevada, including wood, stone, and even ice, were carried down from the mountains to be processed in the city. These goods were brought to Sacramento because of its transportation network; first the river, later the railroads. Sacramento connected California to the rest of the nation. Highway networks converged in Sacramento as well, continuing the city's role as a transportation hub and spurring suburban growth in the mid-20th century. Sacramento's government role grew as the state's population exploded. Today state offices are the employment centers of the central city, instead of factories and food processing plants.

Sacramento's growth in the intervening decades has alternated between upward and outward growth. The first surge upward was simply to stay above water. As agriculture grew to eclipse gold mining in economic importance, a multitude of small farming communities appeared around the old city. Sacramento provided a market for their produce and a place to enjoy the city's entertainments and conveniences, just as miners did during the Gold Rush.

By the end of the 19th century, the original city grid, from the rivers to Alhambra Boulevard (originally Thirty-first Street) and Broadway (originally Y Street), filled with a profusion of homes, increasing the cost of land. Streetcar suburbs, including Oak Park, Land Park, East Sacramento, and Curtis Park, were made possible by horse-drawn and electric streetcars. Suburban residents could afford pleasant homes and ride the streetcar to work. Eventually the city expanded to include these neighborhoods and annexed additional areas as populations shifted. Many of the outlying farm communities later became part of the city, covered with homes instead of crops.

The early 20th century brought upward growth, as advances in building technology and growing affluence brought Sacramento's first skyscrapers and a multitude of civic buildings. Streetcars and interurban railroads helped drive new suburban developments like West Sacramento, North Sacramento, and Colonial Heights. By the 1930s, the automobile became a preferred mode of transportation and streetcars fell from favor. The Great Depression brought much of this new construction to a halt, but some of Sacramento's iconic structures, like the Tower Bridge, were built during those tough economic times.

World War II and the Cold War brought new populations and new industries to Sacramento. Automobile suburbs were constructed to serve military bases and industrial parks located well outside the city limits. Shopping centers and shopping malls were built to serve the needs of these new communities, and freeways simplified commuting to distant suburbs. Some of these suburbs became part of the city, but urban annexation has its limits, and some suburban communities became their own cities. Others remain part of the unincorporated county but with their own community identity.

The old city of Sacramento fell on hard times, the victim of changing economic tides and government policies that favored new suburbs over existing neighborhoods. In the 1950s and 1960s, urban renewal efforts attempted to repair the problems of cities by demolishing their less-desirable areas. City planners tried to attract suburban residents downtown and drive out urban populations through expansion of the central business district, freeway construction, and pedestrian malls. The legacy of urban renewal erased entire neighborhoods, destroying many landmarks and homes. This era also energized a new generation who hoped to preserve the remnants of Sacramento's historic architecture and cultural fabric.

In the 21st century, many American cities are rediscovering their downtowns, and Sacramento is no exception. The city is experiencing a new surge of upward growth, as new buildings appear on its skyline and vacant lots in the central city fill with infill development. Sacramento's urban identity is growing, and many are curious about the history of the old working city of Sacramento.

Then & Now: *Sacramento* is intended to show Sacramento's early growth compared to the present day and provide an introduction to the city's history. Hopefully readers intrigued by these glimpses of the past will seek more histories of the city and will venture into Sacramento's archives and museums, where the buried gold of our city awaits the student of history.

CHAPTER 1

THE OLD CITY

Sacramento City was established to serve the rush of miners heading for the goldfields. The embarcadero along the Sacramento River, just south of the American River, was a convenient place for ships to dock while dropping off men and supplies.

While the city's new site was good for river access, regular floods prompted Sacramentans to build levees and raise the downtown streets to keep the new city above water.

John Sutter founded the first European settlement in the Sacramento region. Before his arrival, the Nisenan tribe lived in the area. In 1839, Sutter selected a patch of high ground near the confluence of the Sacramento and American Rivers for his fort. Sutter named his colony, New Helvetia, after his home country, Switzerland, and coerced the Nisenans to work for him. The discovery of gold on the American River in 1848 cut short Sutter's dreams of empire building.

Sutter left Sacramento in the wake of the Gold Rush, leaving administration of his land to his son, John Sutter Jr. The fort's walls crumbled away, leaving only its central building. When city expansion threatened to demolish the remains of the fort, a civic organization called the Native Sons of the Golden West organized a reconstruction of the historic fort on the site. Today the fort is part of California's State Parks system and a popular tourist attraction.

John Sutter hoped to establish a town on a site called Sutterville, a bluff on the Sacramento River 3 miles south of Sacramento's original city limits. The town did not last long, and by the 1940s, the only building remaining was the abandoned Sutterville Brewery (above). Today the site is just south of the Sacramento Zoo and Land Park on Sutterville Road.

Floods like this one in 1862 (below) were the main reason why Sutter did not select the site of Sacramento for a town. In order to prevent flooding, the people of Sacramento constructed an extensive series of levees. They also elevated their downtown streets by as much as 12 feet above the river level. This pedestrian walkway passes under Interstate 5, descending to Sacramento's original street level.

St. Rose of Lima Church (below) was originally the gift of California governor Peter Burnett to the Catholic Church. The church was demolished in 1887, and the congregation met in a temporary building on Twelfth Street between J and K Streets until the completion of the Cathedral of the Blessed Sacrament in 1889. The old church was replaced by a post office completed in 1894 and demolished in 1967. Because the land was deeded for public use only, the land was rededicated as a park but still bears the name of the old church.

Sacramento became the capital of California in 1854. The county courthouse at Seventh and I Street became the home of the California legislature from February until July 1854, when it was destroyed in a fire. This Classical Revival–style building (above), built on the same site, served as California's capitol from 1855 to 1869, except during the 1862 flood. From January until May 1862, the legislature temporarily reconvened in San Francisco. Today Sacramento's main jail occupies the site.

The Sacramento Valley Railroad (SVRR), completed in 1856, was the first commercial railroad in California. The SVRR was built to carry supplies and passengers from Sacramento's wharves to Folsom, 22 miles away, and to the gold mines. In 1865, this SVRR locomotive (above) was photographed on Central Pacific's tracks at Front and J Streets. Today the California State Railroad Museum's Sacramento Southern Railroad crosses the same intersection. Klamath Northern No. 206 is one of several locomotives used to move equipment around the museum.

The Central Pacific Railroad—the western half of America's first transcontinental railroad—started in Sacramento on the river's embarcadero. Construction began on January 3, 1863, and was completed on May 10, 1869. This passenger depot was built in 1867 and was the western terminus of the transcontinental line. The building was reconstructed in 1976 (above) as the first phase of the California State Railroad Museum.

The city of Sacramento donated a swampy area called China Slough, or Lake Sutter, to Central Pacific if they would fill the swamp. This swamp became the railroad's central shops and locomotive works. When this *c.* 1867 photograph was taken, the first portion of the railroad and its first buildings were perched on pilings (below). The land was slowly filled in over the following decades. Today there is no trace of the swamp, and a handful of buildings remain.

Built in 1857 for Shelton C. Fogus, this mansion at Eighth and N Streets was the home of Leland Stanford, president of the Central Pacific and governor of California. The building also served as a state office building and official residence for Governors Frederick Low and Henry Haight. After Leland's death, his wife Jane Lathrop Stanford donated the building for use as a children's home, a role it played until the 1970s. Today the building is both a museum and California's protocol center.

The Crocker Art Museum was constructed for E. B. Crocker, lead attorney of the Central Pacific, next to his home at Third and O Streets. This expansion was much larger than the original house, intended to hold his family's extensive art collection. The museum is still open and is the oldest continuously operating art museum in the western United States. It is currently undergoing an even larger expansion (below).

In addition to floods, Sacramento suffered devastating fires in the 1850s. Brick houses reduced the risk of fire and for a while were required by city ordinance. Anthony Egl, a fruit and confections wholesaler, built this brick home (below) at 917 G Street in 1860. This house is located in a neighborhood called Alkali Flat, Sacramento's oldest remaining residential neighborhood. Named for the powdery alkaline soil found here, it was conveniently located just north of downtown Sacramento.

This Alkali Flat mansion on Tenth and F Streets was the home of James Neely Johnson, who lived here during his term as governor, from 1856 to 1858. Johnson was 30 years old when he took office and is still the youngest man to become governor of California. A city park next to the house is named after Johnson. Peter Burnett, California's governor from 1849 to 1851, built the house in 1853.

Charles Crocker, one of the Central Pacific Railroad's "Big Four" (the principal owners of the railroad), owned this home at Eighth and F Streets. He supervised the construction of the railroad and claimed that during the six years of its construction he only stayed at this house for about three days. After Crocker moved to San Francisco, his home served temporarily as a hospital for Central Pacific employees. Today the Sacramento County Recorder's Office occupies the site.

This Second Empire Italianate mansion at the corner of Sixteenth and H Streets (right) was built in 1877 for Huntington-Hopkins Hardware Store manager Albert Gallatin. Gallatin later sold the house to Joseph Steffens, who sold the house to the state of California for $32,500 in 1903. From 1903 until 1967, it served as the official state residence for 13 California governors, from George Pardee to Ronald Reagan. Today the final touches of a long-deferred restoration of its exterior are being applied.

DOWNTOWN

Sacramento's downtown business district grew around I, J, K, and L Streets, running from the waterfront to the east. Home to industry, business, government, and retail institutions since the Gold Rush, downtown was also densely populated. Chinese and Japanese communities formed here, and thousands of seasonal agricultural laborers lived in rooming houses and hotels near the waterfront.

The construction of California's current state capitol building took more than a decade. The legislature occupied the building in 1869, even though construction continued until 1874. The original eastern face of the capitol had a prominent, round apse, demolished and replaced by a later expansion of the building in 1952. The original portion of the building was restored and retrofitted for earthquake safety between 1975 and 1981. The trees of Capitol Park surround the capitol building, especially on the eastern side.

Sacramento's city hall at Ninth and I Streets was built in 1910 and designed by prominent architect Rudolph Herold. In 2005, a new city hall building was completed directly behind the old city hall. During the new city hall's construction, archaeological evidence was discovered showing that the site was inhabited as far back as 8,000 years ago. Between the two buildings is a plaza to commemorate the native people who lived here long before Europeans arrived.

The California Pacific Railroad completed their line from Vallejo to Washington (across the river from Sacramento) on November 11, 1868. Crossing the river took over a year, both due to the need for a bridge and Central Pacific Railroad's refusal to allow a crossing over their line at the waterfront. The bridge finally opened on January 29, 1870. Central Pacific purchased California Pacific in August 1871 and used their bridge until replacing it in 1911. The 1911 bridge still stands.

By the 1920s, the Central Pacific (by then known as Southern Pacific) shops had grown into the largest industrial complex in the western United States. Steam locomotives, railroad cars, and equipment of all kinds were constructed here.

To the left of the shops (below) is a passenger depot built in 1879. The open area in front of the shops is the last portion of Sutter Lake to be filled in. Today only seven buildings of the massive shop complex remain.

In 1924, Southern Pacific constructed this new brick depot on the last remaining portion of Lake Sutter. This depot is still in use by Amtrak long-distance and regional commuter trains and is one of the busiest passenger train stations in the United States. Originally served by Sacramento's streetcars, service via light rail trains was reintroduced in December 2006.

Many Chinese came to California during the Gold Rush, and the Central Pacific hired about 12,000 Chinese railroad workers. Many Chinese settled in Sacramento along I and J Streets, in a community called "Yee Fow" or "Second City." The California National Bank (right) was built on the corner of Fourth and J Streets, near the heart of Chinatown. Today the Wong Center (below) stands in the same spot, the tallest building of a two-block redeveloped Chinatown complex built in the 1970s.

J Street was primarily a street of banks, but businesses of all types were found here, like this block between Seventh and Eighth Streets. In the 1980s, a series of fires destroyed most of the buildings seen in this photograph. The last surviving structure, the Coolot Building (above, second from right) was demolished after a fire in 2005. In 2007, a new apartment building, the 800 J Lofts, was completed on the site.

In the 1920s, downtown Sacramento got its first skyscrapers, the Cal-Western Building (below, left) and the Elks Building (below, right). Pacific Gas and Electric streetcars provided commuter service to the business district. R. A. Herold, who designed city hall, also designed the Masonic lodge in front of the Elks Building. Today the Cal-Western and Elks Buildings have much more company in Sacramento's skyline, including the Renaissance Tower, the US Bank Building, and the Robert T. Matsui Federal Courthouse.

Department stores, restaurants, theaters, and specialty shops were found along K Street. For those outside walking distance, local streetcars ran down K Street and interurban trains ran down Eighth Street to bring shoppers from all directions. All of these electric trains passed in front of Samuels Smoke Shop at Eighth and K Streets. Today all of these buildings have been demolished (above). The plans for the resulting vacant lot are in dispute.

K Street was also the home of many elegant hotels, including the Hotel Sacramento and the Hotel Land, and many movie houses like the Fox Senator and the Hippodrome. These hotels are long gone, and all that remains of the Fox Senator is its facade. The Hippodrome Theater reopened as the Crest Theater in 1949 and still operates today. Sacramento's original streetcars ceased operation in 1947, but in 1987, Sacramento's light rail system brought electric transportation back to K Street.

L Street was the southern edge of Sacramento's original downtown district. The Clayton Hotel, built in 1911 (above), was constructed on the former site of the Pacific Water Cure, a hydropathic spa and hospital founded by Dr. Marion Clayton and his wife, Sarah. It was renamed the Marshall Hotel in approximately 1940. Today the Marshall is a residential hotel. There are several of these hotels left downtown. They represent the housing of last resort for many Sacramentans with very limited incomes.

Japanese immigrants came to Sacramento starting in the 1880s and formed a tight-knit community along M Street near the waterfront. Fourth and M Streets, seen here (below), was the heart of the Japanese neighborhood. Today the block from Third to Fourth Streets (above, left) is vacant, and there is no sign of the Japanese neighborhood. A 53-story skyscraper, planned for the site to the left, lost its financing after beginning construction and only a hole marks its presence.

During World War II, many African Americans came to Sacramento seeking work. Some settled along M Street after Sacramento's Japanese Americans were sent to internment camps. Within a few years, an African American community had formed. The Zanzibar Café was one of several popular M Street jazz nightclubs. In the 1950s and 1960s, urban renewal projects demolished the entire neighborhood. State and federal office buildings now dominate M Street, known today as Capitol Avenue (above).

North of downtown at C Street and Eleventh Street, the Globe Mills grain mill was yet another building designed by Sacramento architect Rudolph Herold. This massive, *c.* 1912 concrete building (above, right) was one of several mills that processed grain grown throughout the Central Valley. The mill was abandoned in 1970. Today the structure is undergoing conversion into low-cost housing for senior citizens.

Capt. Frank Ruhstaller, born in Switzerland in 1847, came to California in 1865. He worked in various Sacramento breweries before purchasing the Sacramento City Brewery, shown here (above) at the corner of Twelfth and H Streets in 1881. The offices of the Sacramento Metropolitan Air Quality Management District currently occupy the site.

MIDTOWN

Downtown Sacramento is surrounded by many residential neighborhoods, all part of the original city grid. Here the California State Fair Agricultural Pavilion dominates the eastern edge of Capitol Park, dwarfing the Midtown homes beyond it. The pavilion is long gone, but many Midtown neighborhoods retain their classic architecture and unique character.

Midtown Sacramento is famous for its majestic shade trees. This view of C Street between Nineteenth and Twentieth Streets shows that, aside from a brief interruption for the Western Pacific Railroad's main line, the trees appear to form a solid canopy above the street. Street trees were planted to make walking on Sacramento's sidewalks more bearable in the intense summer heat, a role they still fulfill today.

Memorial Auditorium, at Sixteenth and J Streets, was constructed in 1927 as a multipurpose civic space dedicated to the memory of Sacramentans who had died in the First World War. Used for everything from concerts to graduation ceremonies to sporting events to gubernatorial inauguration ceremonies, the Memorial has undergone significant restoration and stabilization in the past few years.

California's annual state fair was first held in Sacramento in 1855. Sacramento became the permanent site of the fair in 1859, and in 1861, a racetrack for the fair was established between Twentieth, Twenty-second, E, and H Streets. This site, along with the Agricultural Pavilion (pictured on page 43), was the home of the state fair until 1905. After 1905, the real estate firm of Wright and Kimbrough built a new neighborhood, named Boulevard Park, on the racetrack site (below).

This home at 501 Twenty-second Street (below) shows something very seldom seen in Sacramento: snow. On March 14, 1942, Eugene Hepting captured this photograph of the unusual snow flurry. Hepting, one of the racers pictured on page 46 and owner of this house, was an avid cyclist, photographer, and amateur historian who took many of the photographs in this book.

The massive Southern Pacific shops were not the only rail yard in Sacramento. Sacramento Northern (SN), an electric interurban railroad, operated this small yard at Seventeenth and D Streets. Electric freight locomotives, interurban trains, and SN's small Birney streetcars were stored here. SN switched to diesel power in the 1950s and parked their locomotives near this corner until the 1970s. After several decades as a truck unloading area and parking lot, these condominiums (above) were built on top of the SN yard in 2007.

The Poverty Ridge neighborhood got its name from the era when Sacramento flooded often and those living near the waterfront ran to this area of high ground. In the late 19th and early 20th century, when elegant homes were built on the hill, some tried to rename the area "Sutter's Terrace," but the name never stuck. The *c.* 1900 Mason House at Twenty-first and T Streets, near the crest of Poverty Ridge, was built by laundry and haberdashery owner Fred Mason.

Many of Poverty Ridge's mansions have survived, forming the Poverty Ridge Historic District. Others have been replaced by offices or apartment buildings. The home on the left (above) still stands, but the house on the right has been replaced by an office building (below, right). The demolished building was the home of Henry Grau, founder and manager of the Buffalo Brewery.

Henry Grau founded the Buffalo Brewery (below) in 1889 on R Street between Twenty-first and Twenty-second Streets, alongside Southern Pacific's R Street railroad line. Local brewer Frank Ruhstaller became a major partner in Buffalo Brewery in 1897. The brewery went out of business in 1942 and was demolished in 1950. The *Sacramento Bee*, Sacramento's daily newspaper (above), currently occupies the site in a complex built in 1952.

The R Street railroad line was originally the main line of the Sacramento Valley Railroad, purchased by Central Pacific in 1865. R Street was one of Sacramento's principal industrial corridors. On the right (below) is the Carlaw Brothers Stonemasonry lot, where granite from Folsom was dropped off for construction of the state capitol. Today the lot provides parking for the Fox and Goose, a pub located in one of R Street's former industrial buildings.

The largest park in the original city limits other than Capitol Park is Southside Park. A local community group, the Southside Improvement Club, lobbied the city to build the park. Originally occupying eight city blocks, it was completed in 1912. Its principal feature is a large pond originally used for recreational boating and fishing. Today Highway 50 occupies one quarter of the park's area, but the park and the neighborhood remain.

Sacramento's National Guard armory was located on W and Twelfth Streets, near the southern edge of the Southside Park neighborhood. The armory building was demolished in 1965 to make way for Highway 50, which occupies the blocks between W and X Streets through the central city. A new National Guard armory was built at Fifty-eighth Street in East Sacramento.

The Perkins and Company grocery store was constructed in approximately 1910 at the corner of Seventeenth and M Streets. The company was first established in the town of Perkins, a farming community 7 miles east of Sacramento. The Perkins and Company store went out of business in 1944, but the building still serves as a neighborhood market called Rick's Uptown Market (above).

Newbert's Hardware, originally the Newbert Implement Company c. 1925, opened on the corner of Seventeenth and J Streets (below). Store founder William Newbert also played baseball for the Sacramento Altas, one of Sacramento's early baseball teams. Newbert's Hardware closed its doors in 1993. Visible across Seventeenth Street is Sam's Hof Brau. Today Newbert's is occupied by an independent record store, The Beat, and Sam's is now Hamburger Pattie's.

4

STREETCAR SUBURBS

By 1900, Sacramento's population had spilled over its city limits and into several suburban communities just outside of town. The electric streetcar helped promote this growth by providing easy transportation from their workplaces downtown to their suburban homes. These neighborhoods were all later annexed and became part of the city of Sacramento between 1911 and 1964.

Oak Park was the first of Sacramento's streetcar suburbs. Land developer Edwin K. Alsip began the sale of lots in Oak Park in 1887. A streetcar line was built along Sacramento Boulevard, now known as Broadway. In 1910, the Central California Traction Company (CCT) completed an interurban line between Stockton and Sacramento. Their streetcar line served Colonial Heights and Colonial Acres, southeast of Oak Park, and ran through Oak Park on its way to downtown Sacramento. Freight and interurban trains also ran here.

Oak Park featured a neighborhood park on Thirty-fifth Street and Fifth Avenue. The park later became an electric amusement park called Joyland. Here Joyland's Giant Racer roller coaster ride is visible behind the Zig-Zag Alley Shooting Gallery and concession stands (below). Joyland closed after a disastrous fire. The McClatchy family, publishers of the *Sacramento Bee*, later purchased the property and donated the land to the city of Sacramento as a public park called McClatchy Park.

Sacramento City College was a community college first established in 1916. After using temporary quarters at Sacramento High School, this campus on Freeport Boulevard was opened in 1926. The college is located near the neighborhoods of Curtis Park, South Curtis Oaks, and Land Park. In addition to general education, Sacramento City College includes specialized vocational training in aircraft maintenance and railroad operations.

Sacramento's baseball park, home of the Sacramento Solons, was on the corner of Y Street and Riverside Road, south of the city limits. On February 9, 1938, a massive windstorm damaged many trees and buildings in Sacramento, including the ballpark, then known as Cardinal Field. Today a Target store occupies the site. Just south of Cardinal Field were the neighborhoods of Riverside and Homeland. After a large regional park was built in this neighborhood, the area became known as Land Park.

Y Street was originally a levee. After improved flood control made it unnecessary, the levee was removed in the 1920s. In 1938, the Tower Theater was constructed at Sixteenth and Y Streets (above), and the street was renamed Broadway. The long-lasting but now defunct Tower Records store chain got its start in the Tower Drugstore on this corner. In 2008, the Tower Theater is still open, but the drugstore is now the Tower Café.

The Riverside Baths (below) opened in 1909, three miles south of Y Street. Originally an enclosed structure, in 1937 the roof was removed and the baths were renamed the Land Park Plunge. The owners claimed that the baths were fed by Artesian wells. The baths did not allow nonwhites to use the pool, a common practice throughout the United States at the time. In the 1950s, the Plunge was purchased by the Temple B'nai Israel, whose synagogue currently occupies the site.

Just east of Sacramento's city limits on the corner of Thirty-first and K Streets, the Alhambra Theatre was constructed in 1927. Thirty-first Street was renamed Alhambra Boulevard in the theater's honor. Despite its grandeur and strong community support, the theater was demolished in May 1973 to make way for a Safeway supermarket. All that remains of the Alhambra Theatre is a fountain at the southern edge of the parking lot. "Remember the Alhambra" became the rallying cry for Sacramento's preservation community.

East Sacramento began as a streetcar suburb developed by the firm of Wright and Kimbrough and served by the PG&E J Street line. This car line ran down J Street, turned south at Forty-sixth Street, and ran along the eastern edge of East Lawn Cemetery to Elmhurst. Today East Sacramento is known for its elegant homes, especially the area called the "Fabulous Forties." When Gov. Ronald Reagan rejected the old Governor's Mansion, he chose a home in this neighborhood on Forty-fifth Street.

The East Lawn Cemetery, located between Folsom Boulevard and R Street in East Sacramento, opened in 1904. Its mausoleum (above), constructed in 1926, is a community landmark. Prior to becoming a cemetery, the area was known as the Twin Oaks Farm. Two other cemeteries, the Gold Rush-era New Helvetia Cemetery and the Jewish Cemetery, were formerly located in East Sacramento, but both were later relocated.

The home of Julius Gattmann, department store owner and bank director, sits at Thirty-ninth and T Streets, near the entrance of Elmhurst. First developed in 1908, Elmhurst was annexed to Sacramento in 1911. The J Street streetcar line reached the far end of Elmhurst at Forty-sixth and T Streets, but a planned line down the center of T Street to Twenty-eighth Street was never built. Instead, T Street has a broad tree-lined parkway down its center.

Sacramento's county hospital was relocated from Tenth and L Streets to 2315 Stockton Boulevard in 1870. The original hospital burned in 1878. Its replacement was completed in 1879. In 1915, architect Rudolph Herold completed plans for a greatly expanded hospital. This expansion was completed in the late 1920s. The hospital is now known as UC Davis Medical Center. This building (above) is a survivor of the 1920s expansion, surrounded by more modern buildings.

From 1909 to 1967, the California State Fairgrounds were located on a large property at the northeast corner of Stockton Boulevard and Broadway. Served by both PG&E and Central California Traction streetcar lines, this was once the home of the largest state fairgrounds in the United States. In 1968, the fair moved to its current Cal Expo site. This building is one of only a handful of original fairgrounds structures that remain. They are used as city office and medical office buildings today.

Colonial Heights was a streetcar suburb built south of the California State Fairgrounds, along Stockton Boulevard. Central California Traction (CCT), an interurban railroad running from Stockton to Sacramento, entered Sacramento via Stockton Boulevard and operated a local streetcar line to bungalow homes like this one on Fourteenth Avenue. Several of CCT's major stockholders formed the Colonial Investment Company, who built this subdivision. Streetcar service ended in 1946, but CCT operated freight trains along Stockton Boulevard until 1966.

North Sacramento was a streetcar suburb established on the Rancho Del Paso, a large ranch owned by James Ben Ali Haggin. The North Sacramento Land Company purchased and developed a 3,300-acre subdivision named North Sacramento in 1910. This trestle carried Sacramento Northern streetcars between North Sacramento and downtown, in addition to SN's interurban and freight trains. Even in heavy floods, this trestle was above water (below). In 1924, North Sacramento was incorporated as an independent city.

One of the early industries of North Sacramento was the Globe Iron Works. This factory (below) produced, among other things, JN4 Jenny fighter aircraft for the U.S. Army during the First World War. During that era, the facility was renamed Liberty Iron Works. It became one of North Sacramento's major employers. Today some of the Globe buildings are used by a wrecking yard. In 1964, the city of North Sacramento was annexed to the city of Sacramento.

CHAPTER 5

POSTWAR EXPANSION

Sacramento's early suburbs were served by streetcars, but automobiles ruled the suburbs after World War II. Automobile suburbs grew profusely during the 1950s and 1960s. River Park, built along a curve on the American River, was designed as an automobile suburb with wide, gently curved streets. Only two streets lead into or out of the neighborhood.

The McCarty ranch (above) at Fifty-seventh and H Streets was at the outer edge of Sacramento's city limits when Eugene Hepting took this 1938 photograph. In 1849, this area was the northern edge of a farming community called Brighton. Known mainly for its hop fields and pear orchards, Brighton was a stop on the Sacramento Valley Railroad's main line. Today H Street is one of the main arteries of East Sacramento, and the community of Brighton is within the city limits.

This site was once a gravel pit used by the Sacramento Valley Railroad for ballast. Part of the Brighton township at the time, this area was still very rural in 1938 when Eugene Hepting took this photograph along Eastern Avenue (below). Today the street is called Elvas Avenue. A pedestrian underpass beneath the railroad levee, called the "Hornet Tunnel," leads from Elvas Avenue to Sacramento State University.

Sacramento State University, established in 1947, is Sacramento's largest institution of higher learning. It is part of the California State University system. During the floods of 1852–1853, many Sacramentans established a town called Hoboken near the Sacramento State dormitories. Sam Norris, then owner of the land, attempted to establish a permanent settlement, modestly called Norristown, but once the flood waters, subsided everyone else went back to Sacramento.

The H Street Bridge, sometimes called the Fair Oaks Boulevard Bridge, was completed in 1933. This bridge helped connect East Sacramento with the outlying suburbs across the American River. Some of these suburbs were later annexed into the city of Sacramento. Others, like the Arden-Arcade community, are still outside the city limits. Today this bridge supports commuter traffic to and from downtown (below).

Arden Fair Mall was built in several phases, starting in 1957. In 1874, Harris Weinstock and David Lubin founded the Weinstock-Lubin department store on K Street in Sacramento. As shoppers moved to the suburbs, retailers like Weinstock's followed, opening suburban stores like this one at Arden Fair in 1961. The Arden area was annexed to Sacramento in 1962. In 1995, Weinstock's was acquired by Federated Department Stores, and this Weinstock's became a Macy's.

In addition to regional malls, small shopping centers like Fruitridge Manor, located at Stockton Boulevard and Fruitridge Road, appeared in Sacramento's suburbs. As Sacramento's population expanded into new housing developments outside the central city, shoppers preferred driving to nearby shopping centers instead of going all the way downtown. In addition to greater convenience, parking was much easier thanks to suburban shopping centers' ample parking lots. Meanwhile, downtown stores suffered from lack of business.

Florin Mall, built in 1967, was South Sacramento's answer to Arden Fair Mall. Featuring a Weinstock's and a J. C. Penney's, Florin Mall was initially very successful, but hard times came in the 1990s. After losing both of its anchor stores, the mall was demolished in 2006. Today a new shopping center, Florin Towne Centre, is under construction. This shopping center will feature stores near the street, in an open town plan, instead of an enclosed shopping mall surrounded by parking.

About six miles south of downtown Sacramento, a bend in the Sacramento River forms an area known as "The Pocket," originally a farming community. The Sacramento Brick Company, founded in 1854 by John Ryan, had a large clay pit and brickyard here. The photograph above shows the brickyards a few years before the building was dismantled in 1948. Their old clay pit is now known as Greenhaven Lake, and only the street name Brickyard Drive hints at this suburban neighborhood's previous use.

Sacramento Executive Airport, built in 1928, is located about two miles east of the Pocket on Freeport Boulevard. Expanded and reconstructed during World War II, the airport is owned and operated by the city of Sacramento. This control tower and terminal structure was built in 1954. Although it is much smaller than Sacramento International Airport, the region's largest commercial airfield, Sacramento Executive Airport handles tasks including pilot training, charter aircraft, and aerial photography.

CHAPTER

THE UNCITY

During the Cold War era, military bases and industries like the Aerojet complex pictured here drove suburban growth outside city limits. As of 2008, more people live in the "uncity," the unincorporated portions of Sacramento County, than in the city of Sacramento. Some former suburbs are now incorporated cities, including Elk Grove, Folsom, Citrus Heights, and Rancho Cordova.

Town and Country Village, opened in 1946, is one of the oldest shopping centers in California. Developer Jere Strizek used surplus railroad trestles and telephone poles to create a rustic, eclectic destination for the new residents of his subdivisions to the northeast of Sacramento. Displays of tools, firearms, and wagon wheels added to the shopping center's atmosphere. By 1949, 15,000 people lived in Strizek's suburbs. Although remodeling has altered some of Town and Country Village's original charm (above), it is still a community icon.

Farther to the east is the community of Carmichael. Purchased by Daniel W. Carmichael in 1909, the community grew slowly at first. Far from any railroads, improved roads and automobiles spurred growth in Carmichael. Along Fair Oaks Boulevard, about 7 miles from the bridge pictured on page 77, retail stores encouraged commuters to stop. In 1960, the automobile was king on Fair Oaks Boulevard, and little has changed to the present day but the names and styles of the stores.

Country Club Centre, at the corner of Watt Avenue and El Camino Avenue, was built in 1952. The developers, Joseph Blumenfeld and James Cordano, originally planned a drive-in movie theater for the site but later decided that a shopping center would be a better choice. Like many of Sacramento's shopping centers, Country Club Centre was remodeled several times. The name comes from the Del Paso Country Club, located a short distance to the north on Watt Avenue.

Across the street from Country Club Centre is Country Club Plaza. Originally built in 1954, Country Club Plaza shows how far Sacramento's shopping centers had come in the eight years since the opening of Town and Country Village. Instead of trestles purchased as wartime surplus, modern building materials and architectural styles were used (below). Because these styles change rapidly, malls must remodel or risk appearing outdated. Today Country Club Plaza sports an early-21st-century facelift.

The Twelve Mile House (above), on Auburn Boulevard near the border of Citrus Heights, was originally a roadhouse on the old Auburn road. An earlier building was built in 1856, but this building (below) was constructed in 1894. It served as a stop for weary travelers from the Gold Rush era to the years when the Auburn road was part of Highway 40. After the construction of Interstate 80, Twelve Mile House became a neighborhood tavern, finally closing its doors in 1998 after an investor purchased the property.

In 1959, when this photograph (above) was taken, Sunrise Boulevard was still a quiet country road. Citrus Heights was mostly farmland until the 1960s, when the area filled with suburban homes. James Cordano and Ernest Hahn broke ground for Sunrise Mall, near the corner of Sunrise Boulevard and Greenback Way, in 1970. Citrus Heights became an independent city in 1997, and the corner of Sunrise and Greenback is the center of the city's retail district.

The town of Florin, about 8 miles to the southeast of Sacramento's original city limits, was originally settled in 1852. Horticulturist James Rutter and E. B. Crocker, founder of the Crocker Art Museum, purchased 240 acres of land here. Rutter was the first to plant Tokay wine grapes in California. The Frasinetti winery, established in 1897, is the oldest winery in the region. By 1930, Florin was known for its strawberries, and many Japanese farmers had started farms in the community.

Freeport is 9 miles south of Sacramento's original city limits. The town was built by the Sacramento Valley Railroad in 1863. The SVRR's owners had an ongoing feud with the city of Sacramento over taxes. To avoid paying levee taxes, the railroad built a line from Brighton, east of Sacramento, to a new "free port" on the river. The line operated until 1865, when the Central Pacific bought the SVRR and tore out the tracks to Freeport. In 2005, Freeport residents voted against becoming part of Sacramento.

McClellan Air Force Base was established in 1936. It served as a maintenance and overhaul depot for aircraft. It saw considerable expansion during World War II and the Cold War, and its presence spurred development in the surrounding communities of North Highlands, Del Paso Heights, and Carmichael. In 1959, aircraft like this F-106 Delta Dart (below) were maintained here. In 2001, the base was decommissioned and converted to a business park, but National Guard aircraft are still maintained at McClellan Field.

Mather Air Force Base was established in 1918 as a pilot training base. After World War II, Mather became the Air Force's navigation training school and home to a wing of B-52 strategic bombers. Mather was decommissioned in 1993 and today its uses include a civilian airport, a Veterans' Administration hospital, and a business park. The community of Rancho Cordova, established in 1955, is adjacent to Mather, and many residents worked there. Rancho Cordova became an incorporated city in 2003.

The Sacramento Army Signal Depot was technically within Sacramento's city limits, but like any large military base, it functioned as a city unto itself. Originally established in 1942, this military base was first located at the Bercut-Richards cannery on Seventh and North B Streets. Its mission was storage and repair of army communications equipment. This depot on Fruitridge Road was completed in 1945, its home until the base's closure in 1995. Like other decommissioned military bases, part of the depot is now a civilian business park.

The city of West Sacramento, just across the Sacramento River from downtown Sacramento, is actually in Yolo County. Originally settled in the 1800s as several farming communities, West Sacramento was developed as a suburb in the early 20th century and became an incorporated city in 1987. During this 1909 test of a firefighting boat, West Sacramento's waterfront was not very tall. Today the California State Teacher's Retirement System (CalSTRS) building is under construction, next to the distinctive Ziggurat Building (above).

Across America, People are Discovering Something Wonderful. *Their Heritage.*

Arcadia Publishing is the leading local history publisher in the United States. With more than 3,000 titles in print and hundreds of new titles released every year, Arcadia has extensive specialized experience chronicling the history of communities and celebrating America's hidden stories, bringing to life the people, places, and events from the past. To discover the history of other communities across the nation, please visit:

www.arcadiapublishing.com

Customized search tools allow you to find regional history books about the town where you grew up, the cities where your friends and family live, the town where your parents met, or even that retirement spot you've been dreaming about.